Can I tell you about Cerebral Palsy?

Can I tell you about...?

The "Can I tell you about...?" series offers simple introductions to a range of limiting conditions and other issues that affect our lives. Friendly characters invite readers to learn about their experiences, the challenges they face, and how they would like to be helped and supported. These books serve as excellent starting points for family and classroom discussions.

Other subjects covered in the "Can I tell you about...?" series

ADHD

Adoption

Asperger Syndrome

Asthma

Dementia

Dyslexia

Epilepsy

ME/Chronic Fatigue Syndrome

OCD

Parkinson's Disease

Selective Mutism

Stammering/Stuttering

Tourette Syndrome

Can I tell you about Cerebral Palsy?

A guide for friends, family and professionals

MARION STANTON
Illustrated by Katie Stanton

Jessica Kingsley *Publishers*
London and Philadelphia

First published in 2014
by Jessica Kingsley Publishers
73 Collier Street
London N1 9BE, UK
and
400 Market Street, Suite 400
Philadelphia, PA 19106, USA

www.jkp.com

Library of Congress Cataloging in Publication Data
Stanton, Marion, 1956-
Can I tell you about cerebral palsy? : a guide for friends,
family and professionals / Marion Stanton ;
illustrated by Katie Stanton.
pages cm
Audience: 7 plus.
Includes bibliographical references (pages   ).
ISBN 978-1-84905-464-5 (alk. paper)
1. Cerebral palsy--Juvenile literature. I. Stanton, Katie, illustrator. II. Title.
RC388.S73 2014
616.8'36--dc23
2013047818

British Library Cataloguing in Publication Data
A CIP catalogue record for this book is available from the British Library

ISBN 978 1 84905 464 5
eISBN 978 0 85700 850 3

Printed and bound in Great Britain by Bell and Bain Ltd, Glasgow

This book is dedicated to Milly Evans, Adam Lenartowicz and all of the other young people who continue to inspire me with their determination to take their place in the world. It is also dedicated to the memory of Alan Martin who had to wait 31 years to find his voice and used his last 18 years running his own dance workshop business, being a TV star and as a role model not just for disabled young people, but for everyone whose life he touched.

Acknowledgements

Thanks to Helen Dixon, Katie Stanton and Lucy Allen for comments on the text. Also thanks to my editor Lucy Buckroyd for her guidance and support.

Contents

"I want to tell you about cerebral palsy."

"Hello, I'm Sophie. I'm 13 and I have cerebral palsy. I'd like to tell you what it's like to have cerebral palsy. Cerebral palsy is a condition that is caused by damage to the brain when you are born or quite soon after you are born. I didn't know that when I was younger. My mum explained it not long ago. I was born with cerebral palsy because I didn't breathe for some time when I was born. There are lots of different ways that cerebral palsy can affect someone. The main thing is that your brain gets damaged either before you are born, when you are born or in the first couple of years of your life. The brain is the body's controller. It tells the body what to do. If you want to reach out and pick something up, your brain tells your arm to move and your hand to pick up the thing you want. If the bit of your brain that tells you to pick something up is damaged you can think about picking it up, but your arm and your hand just won't behave itself. Just how it behaves depends on what kind of cerebral palsy you have."

"It's great that my friends take the time to wait while I find what I need to say on my communication aid."

"For me, it means I can't talk using my voice and I can't use my arms and legs, but I'm smart. I'm really good at maths and I like science too. I go to an ordinary school and I have an assistant who helps me in class. I have a computer which I use for my work and for communicating with my friends and my teachers. I can do the same work as anyone else but it takes me longer, a lot longer, to write my answers. My friends have learnt to wait when I am talking to them. It can take me a minute to say something they can say in a couple of seconds. They know that they just need to wait and what I want to say will eventually come out. My talking computer is called a voice output communication aid or VOCA for short. It has a posh electronic voice which I like, but other people, especially grown-ups, take a while to get used to it. I must say that I would like it if there was a Geordie accent I could use. My friend Jamie has a Scottish one but they haven't made a Geordie one yet!"

"My friend Dan can't use his hands and he can't use eye gaze technology so he uses a head pointer instead. He jabs the part of the screen he wants to speak out loud with the head pointer."

"Using a VOCA can be a real problem when I meet someone for the first time especially if they aren't used to talking to AAC users. AAC stands for augmentative and alternative communication, and it means that you talk with something else other than speech.

I use my VOCA in two different ways. My favourite way is eye gaze. My VOCA has a camera which picks up where I am looking and if I hold my gaze for long enough the special software will speak out loud the words on the part of the computer screen that I am looking at. I can also use switches, but this is much more tiring and frustrating because I have to wait until a light appears on the choice I want to make and then I have to be quick and choose before the light goes to the next choice. If I miss I have to wait ages for the choice I want to be lit up again. Sometimes though I can't sit in the right position for eye gaze and switches are better than nothing.

Judy runs our after school club. She's got cerebral palsy, but she can walk and talk. Lots of people with cerebral palsy can talk and move easily. Judy has an occupational therapist who helps her to sort out adaptations to her home. She doesn't need many, but special rails in the bathroom help.

My friend Jackie can walk and talk, but she needs to use crutches for long distances."

"Me and Jackie have sleepovers sometimes and we get our PAs to help us dress up and put make-up on. PA stands for personal assistant."

"It's great to have PAs who understand what it's like to want to look good. My favourite PA is Pam and she helps me to choose my own clothes when we go shopping. Pam knows how to do the best hairdos and make-up.

Life has been much more fun since I've been able to be more independent and have my own PAs. They don't treat me like a little girl like Mum and Dad do.

I'll give Mum and Dad one thing: they have been great about me getting to go to sports events. My dad has a sailing boat and he has had it adapted so that I can go sailing with him. I love going to sailing club. I go on a special trip every year with a brilliant group who support children who use communication aids by getting them together for fun events. We have a crazy time and I've made friends in other groups too."

"We go canoeing, abseiling and rock climbing. They have their own zip wire at the centre. My friend Dan goes as well and he is crazy about the zip wire."

"My friend Sally, who also goes on the trip every year, is really into disability rights and she wants to be a spokesperson for the disability rights movement when she grows up. Disability rights are the idea that disabled people should have the same chances to live their lives the way they want to, just like people who are not disabled. She went to Brussels last year as a young spokesperson for The Alliance for Inclusion at the European Parliament. I guess I am pretty impressed with what she did. She and her friends at her mainstream school made a really cool poster about inclusion that they showed to all the politicians who seem to make lots of decisions about our lives. Sally says inclusion is the idea that we all belong in the same place, together."

"My sister Tracy is in the same maths class as this boy called David who has cerebral palsy and is really great at maths."

"David also has his lessons put onto his communication software, so that he doesn't need so much help from his teaching assistants because he can read the questions and write the answers by himself.

Tracy gets David to help her with her algebra. He has the most amazing teaching assistants who make sure he has all the equipment he needs set up just right. He has special software for drawing graphs using the keyboard as a mouse.

I've got another friend, Tom, who was going to mainstream school for half the week, and special school for the other half of the week. He was happier at special school so he started going there full time. Tom has a communication book. It's different from a VOCA. He points to pictures in the book to tell people what he wants to say. There is a boy in his class that uses a VOCA as well."

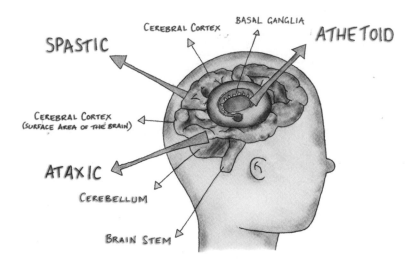

"There are different types of cerebral palsy. It depends which part of the brain is damaged."

"People with spastic cerebral palsy have limbs that don't move very easily. My friend Dan has this. He knows what he wants to do, but his body just won't start moving easily. Sometimes he tries to start a movement for a couple of minutes and then suddenly manages it. When he manages the movement he often makes it to the target. It's different for me because I have athetoid cerebral palsy. When I try to move my arms and legs go all over the place. It's really irritating because I know exactly what I want to do, but my body just won't do as it's told. When I was on my sailing trip weekend there was a girl there who had ataxic cerebral palsy. She walked with a frame but she was all shaky. Judy who runs our after school club can walk and she can pick things up. She can talk as well, but you do need to listen carefully because she slurs a bit. She sometimes drops things as well and can be a bit unsteady on her feet. She has mild athetoid cerebral palsy.

When Mum was explaining about cerebral palsy to me she mentioned a couple of other types. Kids with diplegia have difficulty with their legs, but not so much with their arms and they can usually talk without any difficulty. Those who have hemiplegia are affected in the arm and leg on one side but not the other, or not as much at any rate. Mum says you can have a mixture of any of these kinds of cerebral palsy, so it's all a bit complicated really."

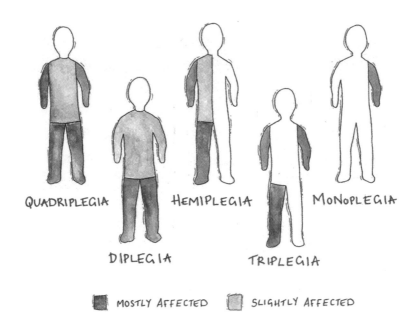

QUADRIPLEGIA   HEMIPLEGIA   MONOPLEGIA

DIPLEGIA   TRIPLEGIA

MOSTLY AFFECTED   SLIGHTLY AFFECTED

"Cerebral palsy can affect different parts of the body. Your whole body might be affected, or just your arms or legs."

"Apparently, you can have learning difficulties too, but I don't. I'm clever even though I can't speak or use my hands. Judy says everyone has strengths and gifts to give. She's right because one girl at youth club who has really severe learning difficulties is the kindest person there and she is always patient and waits while I get my sentence ready on my VOCA. I do sometimes have trouble remembering a word. The words on my VOCA really help with this because I can look around and seeing the word reminds me of the one I want. Mum says it's called word retrieval problems. I am really good at remembering where things are and what they look like. I'm told it means I have a good visual memory.

Quite a lot of people who have cerebral palsy have other problems as well. About half have epilepsy. I just found out that I have absence seizures which are a type of epilepsy that's quite hard to spot. My teaching assistant said I looked like I was glazing over with my eyes still open. The doctor gave me a scan and now I have drugs to control it. I'm not missing what the teacher says any more, but the drugs make me tired sometimes and it can take longer to use my VOCA when I feel like that.

My friend Dan has tonic clonic seizures. He goes all stiff and makes a squealing noise and sometimes goes really red in the face."

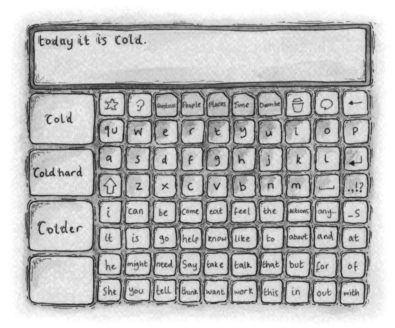

"This is what a communication aid screen looks like. Most people who have cerebral palsy who can't talk need to use communication aids rather than signing."

"Some people with cerebral palsy have problems with hearing or with vision. One girl I know is completely deaf so she has to have a sign interpreter with her all the time.

The doctors gave her a cochlea implant (a tiny electronic gadget placed inside her ear) so she is learning to hear a bit. Tom had a lot of trouble seeing when he was younger. I think they called it cortical visual impairment. This is a vision problem caused by the brain damage being in the area that tells your eyes what they should see. Sometimes it gets better over time but not always.

Sometimes people who have cerebral palsy have emotional or behavioural problems. Others can have problems with spelling and reading even though they are OK with maths. Sleep can be disturbed because it's not always comfortable being unable to move as you want in bed or for other reasons. Going to the toilet might be difficult for some people who have cerebral palsy. They might find it hard to hold it in or difficult to go. I know when I want to go but my muscles don't always hold it in enough. I'm getting better at judging it though."

"My mum needs to help me put on my
AFOs. They help to keep my feet straight."

"I really like my physio Satya. She comes and sees me once a week at home after school. That's when I get to do my best stretches and exercises. She has given me this physio ball that I can lie over and do stretches. Satya has taught my PAs and my mum how to help me with them. She makes sure I have special supportive shoes that look really cool. David has to wear splints called ankle and foot orthoses (AFOs) some of the time and he needs extra big shoes when he is wearing them. AFOs are splints that keep your ankles straight. You can get splints for all sorts of straightening. You can even get a body brace which holds your back straight. Dan went to see a specialist to see if he needed a rod putting in his back to straighten his spine. The specialist decided not to, but some people have an operation for this.

I also have a gastrostomy. This is a tube that goes into my stomach and my PAs give me special milk shakes through the tube that means I keep my weight up. I am much stronger since I had the gastrostomy. Dan finds chewing really difficult, so his food has to be completely whizzed up in a blender to make it smooth. I can chew, but it is hard work so I have some of my meals through the tube and some I eat normally. My PAs chop my food up finely to make it easier."

"Standing is good for my hips. This standing frame helps me."

"Satya comes into school as well, although not every week because that would get in the way of my work. It already takes me four times as long as everyone else to complete my work. Satya sorts out my walking frame but Glen, the occupational therapist, sorts out my standing frame. I need to do some of my work in the standing frame. Satya jokes that the physio is responsible for me from the waist down and the occupational therapist from the waist up. Glen sorts out the positioning of my VOCA on the stand that attaches it to my electric wheelchair. He also sorts out the switches that I need to operate the wheelchair.

All this standing and walking, making my muscles stronger by practising standing, keeps my hips in good shape.

My speech and language therapist is Penny. She comes into school every week and helps me to use my VOCA to communicate. I am planning to take a qualification to show that I use my VOCA well. Penny advises my mum and all the people who help me on the best ways to prepare my food and makes sure that I am eating safely."

"There are lots of other useful therapies such as music therapy, rebound therapy and horse riding. Yes, horse riding can be a therapy. It's also good fun."

"Did you know that kids who were very disabled couldn't even go to school before the 1970s? Unbelievable! They'd either have to stay at home or get sent away from home to a long-stay hospital. Sounds gruesome doesn't it?

Things have really changed. Lots more kids are going to ordinary schools, passing exams and going on to university. My sister's friend David (the one who is good at maths) did a school work placement in a local travel agent and now he wants to get an apprenticeship in one when he leaves school. They said there were loads of jobs he could manage such as counting the money, typing up the cards for the shop window and looking up holiday and travel options for the customers.

There are famous comedians with cerebral palsy – Lee Ridley, Francesca Martinez and Jack Carroll, who nearly won Britain's Got Talent. There's this government fund that helps people who need support to work called 'Access to Work'. Judy told me how it had helped her.

I think that technology is one of the main reasons that opportunities for People with cerebral palsy have got better. I am much better at using Facebook than Mum. Facebook is a great way to talk with your mates without the bother of trying to get the timing right or them having to wait for you to key things into a VOCA."

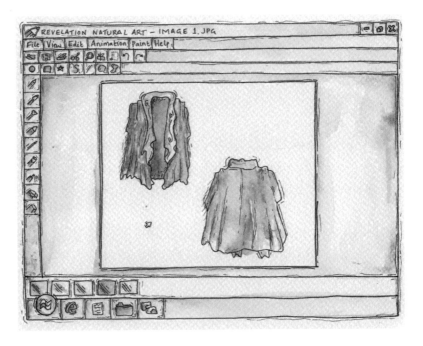

"This is software I can use for design."

"Email, web surfing, Twitter. It's all easier than handwriting and everyone does it so we are really all the same. It's a world where anyone who wants to work from home at their own pace now has a chance, and that means that the future is brighter for people who have cerebral palsy.

I am thinking about how I could start my own fashion business. There are some great software programmes out there that help me to draw and on top of that I could be the brains behind the business, have the ideas and get some of the drawings done by someone else.

Tom can't manage exams because of his learning difficulty, but his special school has this cool scheme called ASDAN which means he can show what he knows in other ways and still get a qualification. I think some mainstream schools are beginning to offer this as well. Tom does lots of practice in life skills at special school. They do lessons in how to have showers and practising using money at the shop."

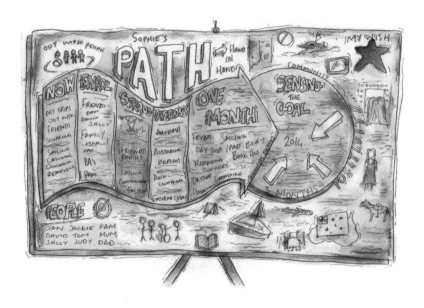

"PATH is Planning Alternative
Tomorrows with Hope."

"I go to mainstream school, which means for me that I concentrate more on my academic work. They are great at helping me to find friends though. When I started a new school when I was 11 they set me up with a circle of support and kids the same age as me were taught how to help me. I got to help the people in my circle by being a good friend to them as well as them helping me. There is this great organisation to teach people about 'person-centred planning'. Everyone should have a person-centred plan. They are brilliant! You spend half a day or a day with all the people who care about you and a trainer who knows how to do a plan. Everything is positive. It's all about what you can do, what you want to achieve, and what help you might need in order to reach your goals.

I wanted to be a hairdresser, but instead of saying I couldn't because I can't use my hands we talked about all the things that would be great about being a hairdresser and what I could do. I can use the computer really well. That means that I can design hair styles and other things and it was the design that really interested me."

"I love going into town by myself
on the accessible bus."

"The trainer in my planning meeting told us about the social model of disability. This is where you don't look at the disabled person as having a problem but the world around them as having the problem. The social model rejects the medical model which is all about what's wrong with disabled people and trying to fix them. In the social model you talk about what people can do to make the world an accessible place, not what the disabled person has to do to fit in. For instance, David likes to go into town by himself without a PA or parent trailing behind him. Well, the bus drivers organised themselves and got ramps for all the local buses so that he can get around. Once when his wheelchair broke down on the bus, the passengers were really nice and helped him to phone home for help without being a bit grumpy about it.

David is doing his exams and he receives support that doesn't give him an advantage but just puts him on a level playing field with non-disabled people who are not up against the same difficulties. He will be allowed to have an electronic reader (that means he can listen to the exam read out on his computer) and a person by him to help him with his equipment."

"A communication passport can be in a book or on a communication aid. If it's on the communication aid it means I can explain about my life using my electronic voice. I have mine in both formats."

"The communication passport tells people basic facts about me like where I come from, who my family are, what I like and don't like and what I hope to do in the future. It is a quick way for someone to get to know me and handy for answering those questions everyone wants to ask about me. The teacher has to look after the whole class, so a teacher who is qualified in AAC and knows about cerebral palsy comes to see me every week. She spends the day with me and my teaching assistants (TAs). Sometimes she comes to lessons to see how I am coping with the curriculum. She also helps me with my writing, reading and spelling using programmes that have been specially written for students who use AAC. She gives my TAs ideas about how to adapt the curriculum, and does some of the adapting herself to give them an example. At my last annual review they talked about it being an ideal model for inclusion. Annual reviews are meetings that are held in school every year to make sure I am getting all the support I need. After the annual review my AAC teacher writes an individual education plan known as an IEP. This outlines goals for my learning and development. My AAC teacher is helping me with my literacy goals of comparing different types of texts. She and Judy work together to support me when I'm updating my communication passport."

"Sometimes my local team of therapists and my school need advice from a specialist centre who know lots about AAC and offer training and assessments. Chris from an organisation that supports people who use AAC visits every couple of months to give me and my team advice. He has helped me to use AAC in lessons, so that sometimes I actually finish a piece of work at the same time as everyone else. They taught my TAs how to adapt the curriculum using special software that I can eye gaze to. My teacher has been on one of their training courses on how to include disabled kids in mainstream school. My mum goes to this big conference every year run by Communication Matters. They are the national organisations supporting people who use AAC and the people who help them."

How teachers can help

- "Plan lessons well in advance and give the plans to my TAs or AAC teacher so that when I get to the lesson I can access it.

- Tell my teaching assistant or my AAC teacher the most important things I need to learn. That way if I get behind I can concentrate on the key points.

- Include me in lessons. I might take a long time to prepare an answer so you can tell me the question you want me to answer at the beginning of the lesson or even before, so that I can prepare my answer. I don't mind if you ask me a question and then ask another question to someone else while I prepare my answer. Don't forget to come back to me though!

- Just because I can't talk doesn't mean that I don't have anything to say. Assume that I understand you and that I have an opinion. Give me time to share it.

- You can usually tell if the work you give me is too easy when I look bored and give a very quick answer. If it's too hard I will probably look lost and confused and not be able to answer no matter how much time you give me.

- A lot of people who have cerebral palsy can walk and talk, but they might still have trouble with writing. Never make a student write who has difficulty with it. They won't be able to think so well. Give them a computer or a simple keyboard like a Neo instead. Sometimes a key guard over the keyboard helps some people.

- Make sure I have the right access method so that I can answer questions and access my lessons in the most effective way possible. Ask an AAC centre or other specialist about this if unsure."

How teaching assistants can help

- "Help me with my equipment and make sure I have a way of giving my answers but please don't help me with the answer. That would be your work and not mine.

- Help me to be as independent as possible.

- Give me time with my friends. If you have to keep an eye on me, please go out of earshot.

- Don't answer for me. If someone asks you a question about me tell the person to ask me directly.

- Don't let people peer at my communication aid display when I am speaking. Encourage people to look at me instead.

- Please let people know what I understand.

- If people want to know more about me I can use my communication passport."

How family can help

- "Include me in things.

- Don't give me unnecessary special attention.

- Let me do ordinary things.

- Find out about leisure activities I can access.

- Try not to get overwhelmed by the huge number of therapists and specialists who seem to be giving advice. If you are finding it difficult to keep up with all the things experts seem to be asking you to do, tell them and ask them for more realistic goals. Suggest they talk to each other if you think the advice you are getting is disjointed or in conflict.

- Remember that having an ordinary life (but a fun one) comes first.

- Listen to my opinion about how I want to be treated and how I want to live my life."

How personal assistants and other carers can help

- "Let me make decisions and not over-ride them wherever possible.

- Be fun and interested in me as a person.

- Try to reach a reasonable balance between my care and therapy needs and my need for an ordinary life."

How others in the community can help

- "Make activities and places as accessible as possible. Ramps and wide doorways can make all the difference to getting around.

- Talk to people with disabilities in a normal way. Treat us like anyone else but make allowances for any extra support we might have.

- Think about what local disabled people might need to join in with community activities and try to make it happen."

How professionals and therapists can help

- "Take our concerns and our families' concerns seriously even if you have different points of view.

- Let us explore alternatives if we ask about them.

- Check regularly that treatments and therapies are really working for us and not impeding our having an ordinary life.

- Talk to each other about what you are advising."

Recommended websites and organisations

UK

General

Scope
6 Market Road
London
N7 9PW
Phone: 0808 800 3333
Email: cphelpline@scope.org.uk
Website: www.scope.org.uk

Offers a wide range of activities to help children and adults who have cerebral palsy including advice, research, holidays, residential care, education and training, assessment, support and information, publications and videos.

Scope's Cerebral Palsy Helpline, 0800 62616, is a free helpline offering information, advice and initial counselling on anything associated with cerebral palsy.

1 Voice – Communicating Together
The Apex
2 Sheriffs Orchard
Coventry
CV1 3PP
Phone: 07943 618 525
Email: via website
Website: www.1voice.info

Contact a Family
170 Tottenham Court Road
London
W1P 0HA

Phone: 020 7383 3555
Email: info@cafamily.org.uk
Website: www.cafamily.org.uk

A national charity which supports families who have children with different disabilities or special needs. It aims to help families to overcome isolation by bringing them together through local mutual support and self-help groups.

Palace for All
The Laundry
Sparsholt Road
London
N19 4EL
Phone: 020 7561 1689
Email: info@palaceforall.org.uk
Website: www.palaceforall.org.uk

Provides play and therapy in an inclusive environment for children with disabilities in north London.

Council on Disability
The Norman MacEwan Centre
(Upper Craigs)
Cameronian Street
Stirling
FK8 2DX
Phone: 01786 462178
Email: codstirling@talktalkbusiness.net
Website: www.council-on-disability.org.uk

Provides information to disabled people resident in Scotland and those working with them.

Disability Action
Portside Business Park
189 Airport Road West
Belfast
BT3 9ED
Phone: 028 9029 7880
Email: hq@disabilityaction.org
Website: www.disabilityaction.org

AAC advice centres
ACE Centre
Phone: 0161 358 0151
Email: enquiries@acecentre.org.uk
Website: http://acecentre.org.uk

NORTH:
Hollinwood Business Centre
Albert Street
Hollinwood
Oldham
Greater Manchester
OL8 3QL

SOUTH:
The Stables
Jericho Farm Barns
Cassington
Oxfordshire
OX29 4SZ
Phone: 01865 759800

Communication and Learning Enterprises
Suite 205
Ulverston Business Centre
25 New Market Street
Ulverston
Cumbria
LA12 7LQ
Phone: 01228 585173
Email: info@candleaac.com
Website: www.candleaac.com

A communication and learning centre specialising in using AAC to support the curriculum and supporting people with complex access needs.

Communication Matters
Catchpell House
Carpet Lane

Edinburgh
EH6 6SP
Phone: 0845 456 8211
(International +44 131 467 7487)
Email: admin@communicationmatters.org.uk
Website: www.communicationmatters.org.uk

The UK umbrella organisation for professionals who work with
people who need AAC.

The Call Centre
Communication Aids for Language and Learning
The University of Edinburgh
Paterson's Land
Holyrood Road
Edinburgh
EH8 8AQ
Phone: 0131 651 6236/6235
Email: call.centre@ed.ac.uk
Website: www.callcentre.education.ed.ac.uk

Provides a range of services for people with communication
disabilities.

Makaton Charity
31 Firwood Drive
Camberley
Surrey
GU15 3QD
Phone: 01276 61390
Email: Mvdp@makaton.org
Website: http://makaton.org

Provides a wide range of resources for parents, carers
and professionals. It helps children and adults with severe
communication and learning disabilities.

Many more assessment centres and other organisations that can
help with AAC can be found at the following websites:
www.communicationmatters.org.uk/resources
www.checkthemap.org

Education

Independent Panel for Special Education Advice
4 Ancient House Mews
Woodbridge
Suffolk
IP12 1DH
Phone: 01394 380518
Email: via website
Website: www.ipsea.org.uk

Provides educational advice for parents of children with special needs.

The Foundation for Conductive Education
The National Institute of Conductive Education
Cannon Hill House
Russell Road
Mosely
Birmingham
B13 8RD
Phone: 0121 442 5556
Email: mmccann@conductive-education.org.uk
Website: www.conductive-education.org.uk

An organisation providing conductive education in this country replicating the methods taught at the Peto Institute in Hungary. Also has further information on conductive education in other parts of the UK.

Advisory Centre for Education (ACE) Ltd
Ic Aberdeen Studios
22 Highbury Grove
London
N5 2DQ
Phone: 020 7704 3370
Email: enquiries@ace-ed.org.uk
Website: www.ace-ed.org.uk

A registered charity offering free advice, service and publications for parents with a focus on school years (5–18) in Local Education Authority schools only. They can advise on many questions parents might have about their children's educational rights and publish very useful and easy to read guides to the law in this area.

AAC City and Guilds
City & Guilds
1 Giltspur Street
London
EC1A 9DD
Phone: 0207 294 2468
Website: www.cityandguilds.com/Courses-and-Qualifications/skills-for-work-and-life/english-mathematics-and-ict-skills/3716-augmentative-and-alternative-communication

Education Otherwise
PO Box 3761
Swindon
SN2 9GT
Phone: 0845 478 6345
Email: via website
Website: www.educationotherwise.net

Supporting people who wish to educate their children other than at school.

London Centre for Children with Cerebral Palsy
54 Muswell Hill
London
N10 3ST
Phone: 020 8444 7242
Email: info@cplondon.org.uk
Website: www.cplondon.org.uk

A school in north London offering conductive education.

Health care and therapy
Whizz-Kidz
1 Warwick Row
London
SW1E 5ER
Phone: 020 7233 6600

Email: info@whizz-kids.org.uk
Website: www.whizz-kidz.org.uk

Aims to improve the quality of life of disabled children in the UK. It provides specialised mobility equipment such as wheelchairs and tricycles.

The Bobath Centre
ENGLAND:
Bradbury House
250 East End Road
London N2 8AU
Phone: 020 8444 3355
Email: info@bobathengland.org.uk
Website: www.bobath.org.uk

WALES:
Bobath Children's Therapy Centre
19 Park Road
Whitchurch
Cardiff
CF14 7BP
Phone: 01292 052 2600
Email: info@bobathwales.org.uk
Website: www.bobathwales.org

SCOTLAND:
Bradbury House
2028 Great Western Road
Knightswood
Glasgow
GI3 2HA
Phone: 0141 950 2922
Email: info@bobathscotland.org.uk
Website: www.bobathscotland.org.uk

Bobath offers a specific physiotherapy programme alongside other therapies.

David Hart
Thorncliffe House
Dawson Road
Keighley
West Yorkshire
BD21 5PH
Phone: 01535 667 306
Email: via website
Website: http://hartwalkermobilitysystems.com/david.htm

At this centre children can be assessed for the use of the David Hart Walker and an after care service is available to ensure that the walker is adapted as necessary with the child's growth.

G.S. Smirthwaite
16 Daneheath Business Park
Heathfield
Newton Abbot
Devon
TQ12 6TL
Phone: 01626 835552
Email: info@smirthwaite.co.uk
Website: www.smirthwaite.co.uk

Suppliers of aids and equipment.

Leisure

Riding for the Disabled Association
Norfolk House
1a Tournament Court
Edgehill Drive
Warwick
CV34 6LG
Phone: 0845 658 1082
Email: info@rda.org.uk
Website: www.rda.org.uk

Listening Books
12 Lant Street
London
SE1 1QH
Phone: 020 7407 9417
Email: info@listening-books.org.uk
Website: www.listening-books.org.uk

Offers a postal audio book service.

Drake Music Project
Drake Music
Rich Mix
35–47 Bethnal Green Road
London
E1 6LA
Phone: 020 7739 5444
Email: info@drakemusic.org
Website: www.drakemusic.org

Enables disabled children and adults who are unable to play
conventional musical instruments to compose and perform their
own music.

British Wheel Sports Foundation
Guttmann Road
Stoke Mandeville
Bucks
HP21 9PP
Phone: 01296 395995
Email: wheelpower@dial.pipex.com
Website: www.britishwheelchairsports.org

Provides training and development facilities for wheelchair users
wishing to participate in sports activities.

Cerebral Palsy Sport
CP Sport England & Wales
5 Heathcoat Building
Nottingham Science Park

University Boulevard
Nottingham
NG7 2QJ
Phone: 0115 925 7027
Email: info@cpsport.org
Website: www.cpsport.org

Co-ordinating body for sport development and competition for people with cerebral palsy.

Disability rights

Parents for Inclusion
336 Brixton Road
London
SW9 7AA
Phone: 020 7738 3888 (office number)
Phone: 0800 652 3145 (free helpline)
Email: info@parentsforinclusion.org
Website: www.parentsforinclusion.org

The Alliance for Inclusive Education
366 Brixton Road
London
SW9 7AA
Phone: 0207 737 6030
Email: info@allfie.org.uk
Website: www.allfie.org.uk

World of Inclusion Ltd
Unit 4X
Leroy House
436 Essex Road
London
N1 3QP
Email: richardrieser@worldofinclusion.com
Website: www.worldofinclusion.com

Training and support with inclusive education.

People First
F173 Riverside Business Park
Haldane Place
London
SW18 4UQ
Phone: 0208 874 1377
Email: general@peoplefirstltd.com
Website: http//:peoplefirstltd.com

A self-advocacy organisation run by and for people with learning difficulties.

Helen Sanderson Associates
34 Broomfield Road
Heaton Moor
Stockport
SK4 4ND
Phone: 0161 442 8271
Email: kerry@helensandersonassociates.co.uk
Website: www.helensandersonassociates.co.uk

Offers person-centred support.

Inclusive Solutions
49 Northcliffe Avenue
Nottingham
NG3 6DA
Phone: 0115 955 6045 or 0115 956 7305
Email: inclusive.solutions@me.com
Website: www.inclusive-solutions.com

Offers person-centred support.

International contacts

USA
The American Association of People with Disabilities
1629 K Street NW
Suite 950
Washington
DC 20006

Phone: 202 457 0046 (V/TTY)
Phone: 800 840 8844 (toll free V/TTY)
Website: www.disabilityresources.org

Disability resources on the internet.

National Disability Rights Network
900 Second Street NE
Suite 211
Washington
DC 20002
Phone: 202 408 9514
TTY: 202 408 9521
Email: info@ndrn.org (general enquiries)
Email: webmaster@ndrn.org (feedback)
Website: www.ndrn.org/index.php

Has information on a number of communication aid centres in
the USA.

Augmentative and Alternative Communication
Website: http://aac.unl.edu/yaack/index.html

United Cerebral Palsy
1660 L Street NW
Suite 700
Washington
DC 20036
Phone: 800 872 5827/202 776 0406
Email: info@ucp.org
Website: http://ucp.org

Inter-American Conductive Education Association
PO Box 3169
Toms River
NJ 08756 3169
USA
Phone: 800 824 2232 (United States only toll-free) or
732 797 2S66
Email: via website
Website: http://iacea.org

Syracuse University School of Education
230 Huntington Hall
Syracuse
NY 13244
Phone: 315 443 4751
Email: dpbiklen@syr.edu
Website: www.inclusioninstitutes.org

Helen Sanderson Associates
850 York Place
Liberty
MO64 068
USA
Phone: 816 781 2505
Email: amandag@helensandersonassociates.com
Website: www.helensandersonassociates.co.uk/about-us/
hsa-usa.aspx

CANADA
Helen Sanderson Associates Canada
736 Lalande Road
Sturgeon Falls
ON
P2B 2V4
Canada
Phone: 705 753 5064
Email: juliem@hsacanada.ca
Website: www.helensandersonassociates.co.uk/about-us/hsa-canada.aspx

AUSTRALIA
Anne McDonald Centre
538 Dandenong Road
Caulfield
VIC 3162
Australia
Phone: 9509 6324
Email: dealcc@vicnet.net.au
Website: www.annemcdonaldcentre.org.au

Offers support with AAC.

Cerebral Palsy Australia
Suzanne Hawes
Scope
830 Whitehorse Road
Box Hill
PO Box 608
VIC 3182
Australia
Phone: 3 9843 2081
Fax: 3 9899 2030
Email: shawes@scopevic.org.au
Website: www.cpaustralia.com.au

The Centre for Cerebral Palsy
PO Box 61
Mount Lawle
WA 6929
Australia
Phone: 08 9443 0211
Phone: 1800 198 263 (country toll free number)
Email: info@tccp.com.au
Website: www.tccp.com.au

Helen Sanderson Associates
PO Box 213
Wallan
VIC 3756
Australia
Phone: 03 5783 4548
Email: info@helensandersonassociates.com.au
Website: www.helensandersonassociates.co.uk/about-us/hsa-australia.aspx

SOUTH AFRICA
Eastern Transvaal Cerebral Palsy Association
PO Box 807
Springs 1560
Website: www.oocities.org/hotsprings/2062

Western Cape Cerebral Palsy Association
Vereniging vir serebraal verlamdes
Box 4267
Cape Town 8000
Website: www.wccpa.org.za

St. Giles Centre
71 Klipfontein Road
Rondebosch
South Africa 7700

United Cerebral Palsy Association of South Africa
PO Box 293
Rosettenville 2130
Phone: 011 435 0386/7/8/9
Email: ucpadmin@netactive.co.za
Website: http://ucpa.za.org

Blank, for your notes

Blank, for your drawings